MW01205098

Become a Handyman

-

A Quick Start Guide

**Start a Successful
Handyman Business Today!**

Bob Cheal

CreateSpace Publishing

**This book is intended to provide practical information about
the subject matter covered, and is designed to help handymen
and women advance themselves in their trade. The materials
in this book are presented with the understanding that the
author renders no legal, accounting, or other professional
service.**

**Consult with your local contractors licensing authority for
information regarding licensing requirements for work that
will be performed.**

*"With thanks to my
very special wife,
Shirley!"*

Table of Contents

5 Steps to Success

What about weekend, holiday or overtime rates?

Should I charge by the hour or by the job?

What if I'm not sure how long a job will take?

What if I run over? When should I charge the customer?

How large a deposit should I request?

How much should I markup the materials that I sell?

Can I get a contractors discount when buying materials?

Should I charge for mileage or travel time?

Should I hire handyman helpers?

5 – Marketing Your Business to Earn Top Dollar for Your Services.........73

How can I set myself apart from my competition?

What type of customer will pay the highest rate for my services?

Should I advertise in the newspaper and the yellow pages?

How can I save on newspaper advertising?

Should I join a professional referral organization?

What other sources of business are there?

Should I get handyman signs for my truck?

Will a web page bring me more business?

Handyman Pricing Guide..............85
How much should I charge for...?

Outdoor Maintenance, Repairs And Installations:

On my first job as a handyman I built this trash can enclosure on the existing pad.

1 - Making the Decision

Are you tired of working for "the man?" If you were laid off, how would you like to have a job where you could never be laid off again? Want more variety in your work? Want more control over your time and the work you do? Want to take vacations whenever you choose? Do you want to be your own boss? Become a handyman!

If you're like me, I considered becoming a handyman for a long time before I actually took the leap. I figured that if things changed for the worse at my job I would pack it in and work for myself. That day came sooner than I thought when the company I worked for closed its doors. One day we were all working comfortably and the next day we were out on the street! I tried looking for another job but it seemed like I was either over qualified or there were no positions open at my experience level.

I asked myself, "Why not start my own handyman business?" I have some tools and I've done lots of light construction. People have always complimented me on being "handy" so why not become a handyman?

Sometimes, the most difficult challenge in starting and running a business is making the initial decision to move ahead! I had a lot of questions...

- How long would it take to get started?
- How much should I charge and how much money would I make?
- Are there too many handymen in my area already?
- What kind of jobs will I be asked to do?
- Would I need a lot of tools?
- How would I market myself?
- What about licensing and insurance, would I be able to protect myself if something went wrong?

- What about bookkeeping and taxes, would they be a nightmare?

My goal is to answer these questions for you. With this Quick Start Guide you won't have to learn the hard way, like I did. You'll be starting off on the right foot!

You will find that it isn't difficult to become a handyman and you don't need to have a lot of top quality tools. But, there is a right way and a wrong way to build your business and you'll discover that the right way leads to a much higher profits for you.

Is there too much competition? You won't be worrying about the competition. If you follow the suggestions in this book you'll be the only handyman your customers will want to talk to.

I've included a Pricing Guide with pictures from actual job sites so that you will have a basis for the estimates you will be making. I've also included a list of many of the jobs that I've completed to illustrate the types of work you might be asked to do.

The "Marketing Your Business to Earn Top Dollar for Your Services" section will show you how to find the best paying, loyal customers and the suggestions on advertising will save you the cost of this book many times over!

Upgraded the lighting in this kitchen by removing the old fashioned light box, re-texturing the sheetrock and installing new light fixtures.

2 - Setting Up Your Business

About Licensing and Insurance

Check with your state or local licensing authority to determine if your handyman work will require a license. To protect your assets it is very important to get the necessary licenses and that you have general liability insurance.

Does a handyman need to have a Contractors License?

There are very few areas where a handyman can get a handyman license, so the question becomes: How can I work legally as a handyman and still make a good living?

It seems that every state in the Union has licensing requirements for all aspects of construction. You have to be a licensed contractor to do any major work...jobs like rewiring a house or remodeling a bathroom. If you are an unlicensed handyman you must look to the exceptions to the licensing requirements. What kind of work can be done without a license?

Most states have some kind of "Minor Work Exemption" rule. There are often maximum dollar amounts for a job or some specific types of work that don't require a license. These exemptions are where the handyman makes his or her money! But guess what? Every state has different rules!

I've found that one state sets the maximum dollar amount for labor and materials at $750, while another is $1,000. Still another state says that you can do up to $3,000 but you have to show that you have liability insurance.

Some states won't let you do any plumbing or electrical work and won't allow you to do any work that requires a permit. It's maddening really. In California, where I live, the limit is $500 but there is an exception which allows the sale or installation of finished products that don't become a fixed part of the structure regardless of the dollar amount. So I can assemble furniture and garage storage cabinets all day long!

Everywhere you go you'll find different rules and it's impossible to quote them here. But they all seem to have one thing in common. They won't let the handyman break the job down into smaller components to make the totals "fit" the rules and the job can't be a part of a bigger job that exceeds the limit.

Obviously the government is trying to protect vulnerable consumers from unscrupulous, unlicensed contractors and they have the minor work exemption rules in their sights as a means of protection. Because of this, we will continue to see the licensing requirements getting tighter and enforcement becoming stricter.

So what is the handyman to do? How does a handyman make a living? Well, we take a closer look at what we are being allowed to do.

We can do repairs all day long. We can do maintenance, we can do minor jobs like installing trim, power washing and staining a deck, doing trash hauling, touching up paint, or minor dry rot repairs, furniture and cabinet assembly. We can repair a fence, build a gate and install a screen door. There are lots of jobs that we can do. In fact, almost everything we can do a licensed contractor will not want to do. The jobs are too small for him to send out a worker. There is a definite niche for a handyman and a great need for honest, reliable handymen and women!

Don't let the licensing limitations stop you. Use them to your advantage. Find partners to work with that will refer you the kind of business you can do.

The years spent as a handyman may count toward your experience requirements if you apply for your contractor's license. Call a local contractors testing school to find out what you can do now to prepare for getting your license. They will also be a great resource for information on what types of work you can do in your area without a license.

Nothing I've said here has stopped me from making a good living as a handyman. Whatever you do, I hope you take away from this question one simple idea. As an unlicensed handyman it's not our job do bathroom or kitchen remodels or to frame out additions. That is not the kind of work we should be looking for and we can't legally build a business based on large jobs.

Who is required to have a city business tax certificate?

If you do work within the city limits, where ever you are, there is probably a business license requirement.

Here is a quote from the City of Santa Rosa's website:

"Any person whose business is located in the city or conducts business in the city must apply for a business tax certificate within 30-days of the date the business commences. Conducting business in Santa Rosa without a business tax certificate can result in penalties, violation notices, citations and court action. Whether you're operating from home or a storefront, office or industrial park, you'll need a Business Tax Certificate."

As you can see, cities are anxious to register your business and collect a business tax! Is your city the same? Fortunately these taxes are usually very small but they do require some extra paperwork.

Go to your city's website or call your city hall. If you're required to have one, bite the bullet and get it for every city in which you will be doing business.

Do I need a Resale Permit and should I use Resale Certificates?

Yes, if you're going to have taxable sales you'll be required to have a Resale or Sellers Permit number and to collect and remit sales taxes to your state.

Upon applying, you will be issued a resale number to be used when filing your sales tax return. You can also file this number with your suppliers (on Resale Certificates) to avoid paying sales tax at the register when making purchases for resale.

I choose not to file Resale Certificates with my suppliers. Because of this, I pay sales tax on my materials even though they will be resold. The benefit to me is that I have a much smaller sales tax bill when I file my sales tax return. Why do I owe less? The reason is simple: my tax liability is smaller because I am credited at the end of the year for all of the sales tax that I paid on those purchases.

For example, if I sold $20,000 of taxable materials to my customers last year at the 7.5% tax rate, I would have collected $1,500 in sales tax from my customers. However, let's say that those purchases for resale cost me $16,000 on which I paid $1,200 in sales tax at the time of purchase. At the end of the year I would only owe $300 in sales tax to the state instead of the $1,500 that I collected from my customers.

$20,000 x 7.5% = $1,500 collected from customers.

$16,000 x 7.5% = $1,200 paid at time of purchase.

$1,500 – $1,200 = $300 sales tax liability.

If you choose to give resale certificates to your suppliers to avoid paying taxes on your purchases you will end up with a larger tax liability at the end of the year ($1,500 vs. $300). Additionally, states base the frequency of your returns on the amount of sales tax due. You may find yourself being asked to file more frequently (quarterly vs. annually). Ugh, that would mean more tax planning and additional paperwork.

One more added complication of purchasing on a resale certificate is that you will be liable for sales tax on any of the tax exempt purchases made for resale that are later withdrawn for personal use. The total purchase price of these items must be tracked and entered into the tax return to correctly calculate your tax liability.

For my business, I've decided to just keep it simple and avoid the use of resale certificates, effectively paying my sales taxes as I go.

Why does a handyman need General Liability insurance?

Insurance is necessary for two important reasons. Insurance will help to protect your assets in case something goes wrong with a job that you complete. Secondly, it will bring you more business. In fact, chances are that it will bring in far more revenue than the cost for coverage.

There are many handymen working in my area and it would surprise me if more than 1 out of 10 carries general liability insurance. The fact that I have insurance sets me apart from my competition and has helped me get additional jobs. I don't hesitate to let people know I have it. "Insured" is on all of my printed materials and business cards.

Having insurance has also opened the commercial market for me. I have done work for professional management companies that have needed small jobs done at their retail stores. One of these companies required that I have at least $1,000,000 in general liability insurance, the second wanted $2,000,000. Interestingly, when I told them about my $1,000,000 coverage limit they still wanted me to do the work. This proved once again that a good handyman (especially one with insurance) is hard to find!

How much coverage should I have?

If my commercial experience is typical, $1,000,000 worth of general liability insurance is a good starting point. On my latest renewal I discovered that raising my limit to $2,000,000 did not increase my premium. Ask your agent for quotes on both coverage limits.

The more assets you have, the more important liability coverage is and the more coverage you need. Please consult your insurance agent for all of the facts. You will also want to get a full explanation of manifestation or sunset clauses when choosing your policy.

Insurance for a handyman is hard to find. Where can I get insurance?

Finding coverage is not always easy, especially if you are a first year handyman. I called around to my local agents and had no luck. On the internet I found an insurance broker who was able to quote a policy for me. You will find a links to insurance agents on my website at Handyman-Quickstart.com.

Do I need to have a catchy name for my handyman business?

If you're interested in selling your business down the road you will want to have a catchy name. It would be pretty tough to sell Jim Smith's Handyman Service to Jenny Jones!

But there are some downsides. Using a fictitious name (any name that isn't your given name) will cost you some extra money. Once you've chosen the name you'll be required to register that name with the local authorities and to pay to publish the announcement of the name. You'll probably want to have a logo to go along with your new name too and that could mean additional expenses.

This is the route that I chose to take, but in retrospect I could have just used my given name and added "Handyman" as my title. Besides saving on the cost of the filings and the extra time involved getting the paperwork together, I wouldn't be on every credit card company's mailing list under my business name!

Regardless of the name you choose, business cards are a must. There are some great online print sources for professional looking cards listed on the Resources and Helpful Links section my website: Handyman-Quickstart.com. You can lay out the cards online to save on graphics fees.

Order plenty of cards and give them out to everyone you know. When someone asks for my card I always give them three so they have one to keep and two to pass on.

Do I need an email address and my own domain name?

Yes on both counts. An email address and a domain name will help to build your credibility. They prove that you are serious about your work and give your clients another way to communicate with you.

I encourage you to get your own personalized domain name and use it for your email address and your webpage. There are many free email services and free web hosting services out there and you may be tempted to save money by choosing one of these. Before doing that, consider these two email addresses:

bob@shipshapehome.com vs. bob2445@yahoo.com

Who would you rather do business with?

What legal business structure should I choose?

The three most commonly chosen legal business structures are Sole Proprietorship, Limited Liability Company (LLC), and S Corporation. Because I am not a lawyer or a tax attorney I am not qualified to recommend one structure over another. I can only tell you what I have done and strongly recommend that you consult with an attorney and an accountant before making your final decision.

I chose the simplest and most basic structure you could set up, with all of its benefits and pitfalls - the Sole Proprietorship. As a Sole Proprietor income is reported on the individual income tax return (1040, Schedule C) so there is very little additional paperwork. If you choose this option you represent the company legally and fully and you are personally liable for all debts and actions of the company. If something went drastically wrong with a job you completed your assets could be at risk. This makes it very important to carry sufficient liability insurance.

I suggest you seriously consider forming an LLC, particularly if you have a lot of personal assets and/or will be hiring employees. Since the handyman trade could be considered a high risk industry, many handymen choose this option. This structure affords the members (owners) the liability protection of a corporation. Unfortunately, this liability protection may not be complete as you could still be held personally liable for your actions if you have signed a personal guarantee. Personal guarantees are often required by banking institutions if you get a business loan.

A third option, often chosen by contractors is the S Corporation (Small Business Corporation). This structure allows the profits to be taxed in a way similar to a Sole Proprietorship avoiding the double taxation problem inherent to the corporate system. As with the LLC, the presence of a personal guarantee would leave the owners personally responsible for debts.

For inexpensive legal advice I became a member of Pre-Paid Legal Services. This is an extremely low cost legal service that I have found to be a great asset. For less than $20 per month you have legal advice that is just a phone call away. It's a lot like having a lawyer on your payroll! Pre-Paid Legal associates are easy to find and they will be glad to sign you up.

About Record Keeping and Taxes

Federal income taxes, state income taxes, city business license tax, sales tax, payroll taxes, wow! Taxes and recordkeeping can be quite a load.

Your record keeping will make or break your business success. Setting your books up correctly from the start will make everything easier when it becomes time to prepare your taxes.

Here are some keys to success:

- ✓ Open a separate checking and savings account for your business.

- ✓ Get a new visa card strictly for your business use.

✓ Keep all of your receipts, job invoices and bank statements.

✓ Purchase a box of file folders to store your receipts, invoices and bank statements. Keep them in a file drawer or file storage box organized one folder for each month.

✓ Keep separate files for insurance, sales tax, business taxes, and licensing.

✓ Maintain mileage logs reflecting odometer readings and job names.

✓ Use a computer based bookkeeping system and set up your chart of accounts as shown below.

✓ Keep on top of your bookkeeping. Don't let it pile up!

✓ Be aware of the different sales tax rates you may have in your area. In my immediate vicinity there are four different sales tax rates. Because of this, I keep track of my sales by area. This helps tremendously when the time comes to complete the sales tax return!

I do all my own bookkeeping and file the returns myself. I use Quicken® because it is inexpensive and easy to use. Any bookkeeping system should help you successfully track income and expenses and easily complete your taxes.

Do I need an accountant and a bookkeeper?

Unless you've had a lot of experience with taxes, you may want to have a tax preparer complete your first year's tax returns. In subsequent years you can often prepare your own taxes by following last year's example.

I have found that after the chart of accounts has been set up properly your bookkeeping system simply requires maintenance. Bookkeeping software has greatly simplified this once difficult task and has made it possible for someone like myself, who has moderate bookkeeping and tax experience, to do it myself.

Alternatively, you may have a spouse or partner available to do the bookkeeping. If their time permits, in addition to preparing the deposits and paying the bills, they could answer incoming phone calls, contact clients regarding scheduling and make follow-up calls. Your time would be freed up to make estimates and complete more jobs. This arrangement could ultimately translate into better customer service for your clients and more income for you both.

The most important thing is that the bookkeeping and taxes be prepared accurately and on time. Accountants and tax preparers are called experts for a reason, bring them in if you need advice and to save yourself time and aggravation.

What should my chart of accounts look like?

Since the 1040 Schedule C is your basic profit and loss statement, I set up my chart of accounts to match the Schedule C as closely as possible. You should need very few categories that aren't listed on the Schedule C. If your state has a sales tax and you have differing tax rates in your area you should break down your sales by tax region. Also, keep track of tax paid on materials purchases by tax region.

Here is my chart of accounts:

Income Accounts:

Labor Sales
    (Broken down by sales tax region)
Materials Sales
    (Broken down by sales tax region)
Sales Tax Collected
    (Broken down by sales tax region)

Expense Accounts:

Advertising
Car and Truck
Contract Labor
Insurance
Interest
Legal and Professional
Office Expense
Equipment Rental
Repairs
Supplies (Not Cost of Goods Sold)
Purchases: (Cost of Goods Sold)
  Tax Paid Purchases
    (Broken down by sales tax region)
  Non-Tax Paid Purchases
    (Broken down by sales tax region)
Taxes and Licenses
Entertainment
Employee Wages: (If you hire employees)
      Wages
      Federal Tax Withholding
      State Tax Withholding
      Medicare
      FICA
      SDI (Disability Insurance)
Other Expenses

Do I need to keep a mileage log?

Yes. At the time of this writing, IRS Form 2106 instructions (for 2008 returns) had this to say about record keeping for your vehicle: "You cannot deduct expenses for travel…unless you keep records to prove the time, place, (and) business purpose…of these expenses."

I keep a small spiral notebook in the visor of my truck. Each morning I list the names of the jobs I'll be doing and the current odometer reading. As I go from job to job, I record the odometer reading. At the end of the month, this page is torn from the book and added to the file that I keep for each month's receipts. (Every month has its own folder.) When matched with invoices these logs serve as my written record of mileage and business purpose.

In the same spiral notebook; record the money you spend for gas, insurance, registration, maintenance and repairs of the vehicle. Save your receipts. At year end you will decide whether to take the standard mileage rate or actual expenses on your taxes. Check the tax codes for limitations and for the current mileage deduction rates.

Are labor and materials sales subject to sales tax?

Since every state has different guidelines, the best suggestion I can make is to use the local state sales tax office as a resource and follow their instructions to the letter. I am lucky enough to have a state office located in our city so I opened my account in person and asked a lot of questions.

Collecting the correct sales tax can be tricky and the rules are full of pitfalls. Is labor taxable? What about materials sales? If you tell someone that the cost of the job will be $500 is the entire amount subject to sales tax or just the portion that covered the materials?

If both your materials and labor are taxable your sales tax liability will be MUCH higher. In my business, labor accounts for about 85% of my total revenue.

In California, because labor is generally not taxable and materials sales are, you have to be very careful how you quote prices and fill out your invoices. You must clearly break materials out from labor when quoting the work and while totaling the invoice or you might be liable for sales tax on the entire sale. I always quote labor and materials as separate items.

How should I manage my money for taxes?

Many business people have found that in their first year in business, the biggest challenge is keeping the doors open and paying the bills. The second year another problem arises...how to pay all of the income tax! Because there is a lot more money flowing in the second year they find themselves spending too much and having too much fun. Unfortunately they don't foresee how large the impact of taxes can be and don't set enough aside for taxes.

The good news is that your overhead as a handyman is low and you should be earning a profit early on. The bad news is that you will need to plan for taxes right from the beginning. The best way to handle this is with a savings account specifically for taxes. Every time you deposit your earnings, deposit 20% of the total into your tax savings account. Yes...20%. Want a different number? An alternative is to transfer funds at month end after you've closed your books and calculated your profits. Transfer at least 35% of your net profit after expenses.

I know from experience that this is not easy. So whatever you do, make deposits regularly into your tax savings account. Use these funds to make quarterly estimated tax payments to the IRS and to your state.

Quarterly tax payments?!? Yes, otherwise known as Estimated Tax Payments, these are a sad reality of working for yourself. These are the equivalent of withholding from your paychecks. The federal government and most states want to be paid throughout the year, not just at the end. They'll penalize you if you don't make payments at least four times a year. (IRS due dates are Apr 15, June 15, Sept 15, Jan 15)

The percentages I've given are obviously an estimate. Unfortunately, you may not know exactly how much you need until it is too late so save all that you can and as often as possible.

If you've been generous with your tax savings account you will find that the estimated tax payments won't be so painful after all. At year end, after your income and sales taxes are paid, you may even have money left for that hard earned vacation. It'll be just like getting an income tax refund!

Can a handyman open a SEP-IRA retirement account?

According to the IRS; businesses, corporations and self-employed individuals can open retirement accounts including the SEP-IRA. As a self-employed person the amount you can contribute is dependent on your profit for the year.

It is not easy to calculate your allowable contribution. Always looking for a bargain, I opened a SEP-IRA at one of the large discount mutual fund families. Their retirement planning department was great about answering my questions, they calculated my allowable contribution and all of their advice was free! Check with a tax professional or a financial planner to see if you qualify.

About Invoicing and Billing

To promote a professional image and set yourself apart from your competition, you must use a professional looking invoice. Customers appreciate having a paid invoice and you will find that all commercial work will require it. The invoice that I use carries my logo, name and address, and has a place for the customer to sign that they have accepted the job as completed. I leave a copy with the customer and keep the signed top copy for my files.

You will find an invoice template on my website at Handyman-Quickstart.com. Print out the template; paste your logo at the top left and your name and address into the top right box and take it to your local full service copy store. Have them create 2 part NCR (no carbon required) forms. You should end up with 200 invoices for around $50. This is a real bargain when you consider the level of professionalism you just added. If you will be doing commercial work, you should consider having the invoices printed with sequential numbering. The numbering can be done at the time the NCR forms are printed. Aluminum invoice boxes can be purchased at office supply stores to hold your invoices.

Should I accept credit cards?

I haven't had a single customer ask if I accept credit cards. I don't think they expect me to. Because of the cost, approximately $25 per month for the merchant account plus the transaction fees, I have decided not to take the leap.

However, there are some compelling reasons to accept credit cards. It is great to be able to offer the credit card option to the rare customer who, after the work is done, says that they don't have the money. If you have a merchant account you can let them charge it!

Secondly, by letting your customers know that you accept credit or debit cards you will set yourself apart from your competition. Every advantage helps.

Here is the least expensive way to accept credit cards. Open a Paypal business account. Your customers can pay with their charge cards even if they don't have a Paypal account. The fees charged to you are minimal and are strictly on a per transaction basis. There are no monthly service fees. Your customers could also pay with their Paypal account. Visit the Resources and Helpful Links section on my website: Handyman-Quickstart.com for more details.

What about billing customers for completed work?

If it brings you more business, just say "Yes." This has come up in three different situations. When I've done commercial work, work for a property management company or while doing pest repairs for real estate agents.

The problem with billing customers on account is the time delay in receiving payment. Commercial accounts often take up to 90 days to pay and require extra paperwork when requesting payment. Completed pest work is often paid through escrow when the house is sold and can take 30-45 days for receipt. In all cases, the submitted bill has proven to be as good as money in the bank but you must allow for the extra time.

Should I accept personal checks?

Yes! Most customers pay by check. However, when in doubt do what the corner merchant does to cover himself. Write the customer's driver's license number on the check to prove you checked their ID. In order for the police to help you collect on a bad check, you will need to be able to prove who it was that signed the check.

Should I ask to be paid in cash?

No. Never tell a customer that you prefer to be paid in cash. Asking for cash is bad business and a dead give away that you are cheating on your taxes.

What about Preliminary Notices and Mechanics Liens?

Here is a definition for you: A Preliminary Notice contains language which describes the details of the contract and who the interested parties are to the transaction. It also makes a statement to the property owner that a mechanics lien could be placed on the subject property, what the consequences of such a lien placement are, and what their remedies would be. The placement of a Mechanics Lien helps to ensure that you receive payment for your services. The owner of the property will not have clear title until the lien is released.

I've never filed a Preliminary Notice or a Mechanics Lien for work that I've done as a handyman. Would I be sorry that I hadn't? Yes, if I'd done work for a homeowner or a contractor and never got paid!

As a handyman, we continually work under the assumption that we will be paid for the work that we do. If payment is never received, the homeowner has great leverage against us. It is usually impossible to repossess the work that we did.

A Mechanics Lien is our way of insuring that we receive payment. The Preliminary Notice is the first step in the process and it lets the homeowner know that a Mechanics Lien could be filed. This in itself is often sufficient to prompt the homeowner to pay for the work making the actual filing of the mechanics lien unnecessary.

Check your local authorities for details. Each state has its own filing requirements, time restrictions and laws.

3 – Truck and Tools

Does the truck I drive really matter?

Yes! A handyman's truck should tell the world that they are dealing with a reasonably priced professional. It should indicate to your customers that the owner is clean, organized, efficient, and serious about their work.

Buy a good used truck or a basic new truck like I did. Don't get anything too flashy because it will make you look too successful. Better to be simply clean and reliable. A little extra fuel economy doesn't hurt either (I drive about 1,200 miles per month).

The picture above shows my truck. I carry nearly all of my tools with me. This has proven to be a good practice because it enables me to do the unexpected job and reduces the "I don't have the right tool" frustration factor. In order to do this, I needed a truck with a shell or a tool van. As you can see, I chose a small pickup with a standard shell and a small rack on the roof.

The disadvantages of my set up are probably clear to you. First, the rack on top is too light to carry large lumber loads. A standard rack would have been a better choice. I continue to manage with this small rack but I am often pushing tools aside in the bed to make room for lumber.

Next, the camper shell should have been a workman's shell with side access to the bed. That would save a lot of crawling into the bed to retrieve items stored toward the front of the vehicle. A workman's shell would also be more secure with stronger locks and no windows.

What tools does a handyman need?

You don't need a long list of tools! To get my business off the ground I bought one of the 4-piece, 18 volt cordless tool sets. When combined with the small box of tools I already owned, I was in business! It was that easy.

The tools you need will be dependent on the types of work you take on. Here is my tool collection:

I carry these tools in the truck with me at all times:

- ✓ 6 ½" Cordless Circular Saw
- ✓ 3/8" Cordless Drill
- ✓ Cordless Reciprocating Saw
- ✓ Cordless Flashlight
- ✓ Detail Sander
- ✓ Corded Planer
- ✓ Cordless Shop Vacuum
- ✓ Corded Circular Saw
- ✓ Corded Jig Saw
- ✓ 6' Step Ladder
- ✓ 8" and 36" Levels
- ✓ Stud Finder
- ✓ Continuity Tester and Volt/Amp Meter
- ✓ Hacksaw
- ✓ Miter Saw and Block
- ✓ Tool Belt

✓ Eye and ear protection, dust masks, knee pads and latex gloves.

✓ A small 5 drawer tool cabinet with all the common hand tools including a hammer, screw drivers, pliers, chisels, files, squares, wrenches, vise grips, tin snips, Allen wrenches and paint scrapers. The top drawer has compartments and a lid so it can carry all of the nails, screws, drywall inserts, wire nuts and most of the other miscellaneous small parts that I need. The second drawer holds all of my screwdrivers while the third drawer carries wrenches, pliers and drill bits. The next drawer has sandpaper, files, scrapers and spare blades. The deeper bottom drawer holds my hammer, squares, super bar, cat's paw and a pouch with my continuity tester and stud finder. This small chest has proven to be the perfect tool box to keep me organized and it is not too heavy to lift in and out of the truck.

✓ A tool box with painting supplies.

✓ An additional tool box with tools for plumbing.

✓ Large covered plastic storage bin to carry all of the extra parts that tend to accumulate.

✓ Three 5 gallon buckets. One holds tubes of caulk and adhesives, another holds anything too long to fit in the tool box and the last bucket is for trash! I also carry a can of Latex Primer and a roll of paper towels at all times.

✓ 50′ Extension Cord

These tools I carry as needed:

✓ 4′ and 8′ Step Ladders

✓ 20′ Extension Ladder

✓ 48″ Level

✓ Collapsible Saw Horses

✓ 10″ Chop Saw

✓ Cordless Finish Nail Gun

✓ Plunge Router

✓ 2650 PSI Pressure Washer

✓ Lawn Mower

✓ Trimmer

✓ Shovel

✓ Rake

✓ Post Hole Digger

Don't let a lack of tools keep you from getting started as a handyman. Using the money you earn along the way, build your tool collection as the needs arise.

When should I rent tools instead of buying them?

A Case Study: A pressure washer is readily available from an equipment rental yard. The first time I needed one, in order to save on the rental fee, I borrowed a pressure washer from another handyman. He instructed me in all the intricacies of getting it started. After pulling the cord about 20 times and fiddling with the controls, it finally started and I got the job done. Whew!

The next time, I rented a machine at a cost of $60. It also proved difficult to start, but even worse, after about 10 minutes it quit and refused to start again! I hauled it back to the rental store for a replacement and finally finished the job. It took me twice as long as I had planned. Time lost equals money lost.

I decided to buy my own machine. Purchased online it arrived at my doorstep for about $400. It was shiny and new and had a Honda engine. That engine started on the first pull and has never let me down.

Rent vs. buy? If you need the machine frequently, buy it. Think of it as an investment instead of an expense! If you're only going to use a machine once or twice a year, rent it and cross your fingers.

I have recovered the cost of my pressure washer by charging a $45 machine fee on every pressure washing job I do. The fee covers gas, maintenance and wear and tear. You could easily do the same with any specialized equipment that you use.

What jobs are handymen being asked to do?

Here is a partial list of the jobs I completed over a recent 4 month period. I'm sure that you will be asked to do the same types of work:

- Installed phone extension line

- Hauled old wood and irrigation pipe to the dump

- Repaired and replaced broken sprinkler heads

- Sealed cracks in brick walkway

- Bleached and stained deck

- Installed closet pulls

- Painted gutters and downspouts

- Moved furniture from room to room

- Repaired a fence post and gate

- Cleaned gutters

- Installed linoleum floor tiles

- Repaired a water-damaged bathroom floor

- Patched, textured and painted sheetrock

- Installed bathroom window coverings

- Replaced damaged window trim

- Replaced weather-stripping on front door

- Installed tubular skylights

- Touched-up paint on popcorn ceiling

- Power washed house in preparation for painting

- Repaired damaged commercial fascia boards

- Installed new kitchen drawer slides

- Replaced damaged baseboard

- Hauled a couch and old cupboards to dump

- Power-washed and applied stain to decking

- Installed earthquake strapping for water heater

- Painted a garage door

- Repaired drip irrigation system

- Built a short flagstone walk

- Spread bark and pea gravel

- Stripped, sanded and painted damaged fascia boards
- Mowed and weeded for bi-weekly client
- Installed a ceiling fan
- Replaced a bathroom faucet
- Replaced an attic ventilator fan
- Completed Section 1 dry rot repairs at the base of a shower
- Sanded, primed and painted an outdoor railing
- Painted walls and trim, repaired closet doors
- Fabricated and installed missing clip for fireplace doors
- Installed a wall air conditioning unit
- Stabilized loose thresholds
- Replaced leaking outdoor faucet
- Replaced rotted wooden ramp
- Built new stairway for a deck
- Replaced screening for door and window
- Painted a bedroom

- Laid a moisture barrier in crawl space
- Installed grab bars in a shower
- Installed smoke detectors
- Cut and installed dowels for sliding windows
- Replaced worn out door hardware
- Replaced washing machine supply valves
- Removed and disposed of a large metal awning
- Disassembled and disposed of a huge garage shelving unit
- Cleaned gutters and installed gutter guard
- Reattached drooping heat duct in a crawl space
- Hung 2 large paintings on a high wall over a staircase
- Hooked up washer and dryer units
- Replaced wax ring and secured toilet
- Installed air hose system for a furniture repair shop
- Dry rot repairs on a front porch pillar
- Installed a new lock on a gate

- Corrected an installation of irrigation valves done by another handyman
- Replaced roof on a 14' diameter redwood water storage tank
- Replaced a room thermostat
- Built and installed a new door for hot tub
- Sanded and stained a shelving unit
- Repaired paneling on a water damaged patio
- Painted front trim and front door
- Replaced worn out toilet valve
- Replaced buckling siding and referred client to a foundation specialist
- Installed a new threshold
- Installed kitchen base molding
- Removed and replaced blower motor for a church pipe organ
- Replaced an inefficient light fixture
- Caulked around a tub, shower, sink and toilet
- Added a new porch light

- Re-hung a loose chandelier

- Adjusted sticking closet doors

- Installed a new front screen door

- Installed a new mailbox and post

- Painted garage walls

- Caulked dissimilar joints around exterior of house

- Built and installed a bathroom shelf

- Rat-proofed the perimeter of a home

- Built a chicken coop

Should I specialize in one type of work?

After viewing the long list of projects above, you might be motivated to specialize in one particular type of work. I have been tempted to specialize because it is challenging to do so many different types of work. On some jobs I find myself learning as I go and having to excessively focus on avoiding mistakes or wasting materials.

When you specialize in a particular area you gain economies of scale on your materials purchases. This improves your profit margins. At the same time you minimize the cost of tools and equipment needed. The work that you do becomes second nature and the learning curve for your helpers shortens.

Choose a specialty that has high demand and that you enjoy. Your biggest challenges and your best earnings come when tackling the most demanding jobs in your area of expertise. These are the jobs that only you, the expert, can do. Pest repairs, pressure washing, painting, landscaping, disaster preparedness, alternative energy, light carpentry, fence repairs, telephone and network wiring or home theater wiring are just a few examples.

Replaced roof on a 14′ Redwood Water Storage Tank

4 - Setting Your Prices

When I first considered becoming a handyman I asked myself, "How much can I earn as a handyman and can I charge enough to make a decent living?" I proceeded to scour the internet to see what other handymen were charging for their services.

The rates being charged were all over the board. Some handymen quoted hourly rates on their websites and some quoted job rates. Some quoted rates for every small job you could think of while others didn't quote any rates at all. More than one handyman quoted additional weekend, holiday and overtime charges as if he was trying to cover himself for any eventuality. It became obvious that there are regional differences with some areas as low as $20 per hour and some as high as $75 per hour.

Overall I was encouraged by what I found. My goal was to earn a decent living and be paid fairly for the work that I performed. The rates being quoted by the most professional handymen/women were high enough that I thought it would be possible to make good money. But the next question came to mind...

What should my hourly rate be?

My web search yielded no local handyman rates so I continued my search the old fashioned way...I started asking around. I know some real estate agents in the area and I asked them if they knew any handymen, and how much they charged.

From their referrals, I talked to a handyman who had a good reputation with these agents. He told me that he quoted $25 per hour. I thought it was too low for our area. He also told me that he would send some of his business my way because he was too busy to handle it all. Now I knew he was definitely undercharging!

The laws of supply and demand should have driven his rates up, yet he claimed that he had been charging the same rate for the last 15 years. He hadn't raised his rates because he didn't want to upset his long time customers.

This example showed me how important it is to choose your rates carefully. It will be more difficult to raise your rates later, particularly when you are getting a lot of referrals from current customers.

You don't have to price yourself cheaply when there is plenty of business available. Another handyman I talked to had all the business he could handle and charged $50 per hour. He presents himself well and receives lots of referrals.

To take this project a step further I researched a handyman franchise in our area. I found that they are charging $115 per hour and have a 2 hour minimum! Are they too busy also? I don't think so. In fact, they had a booth at the last Home Show I attended. There they were, hawking their services and showing off their beautiful marketing materials. Clearly, their challenge is finding enough customers who are willing to pay extra for a professional licensed handyman. Perception is everything and the handyman franchises are doing a great job of cashing in on their professional image.

With this sampling of rates I had a starting point. Not having high overhead, I knew I didn't need to charge as much as the handyman franchises. Since I've never been a big fan of working long hours and earning less than I'm worth, I decided that I didn't want to start too low either! If I could maintain a professional image and do good work, why not try for a higher rate? If I charge less then the major franchises I'll still be seen as an inexpensive alternative.

I decided to start out charging $60 for the first hour and $45 per hour thereafter. I correctly guessed that my customers would be willing to pay my rate. I also knew that I could offer a discount to my rate as a 'special' or even knock off some time when totaling up the invoice if I felt I should.

Do the same research in your area and don't hesitate to push the envelope. What ever your local rates are, there will always be a low rate set by the wannabes, a middle rate set by the professionals and a high rate set by the franchises. Position yourself as a professional by setting your rates at or above the middle and below the top. You don't need to be the cheapest handyman in town to get all the business you need!

Should I offer senior and group discounts?

Yes. Offer seniors and non-profit groups a discount rate. When friends and former co-workers approach you with work offer them a discount rate too. There is great demand in the senior community and non-profit groups for reasonably priced work and, if you deliver on your promises, will be glad to pass your card on to their friends. The Board of Trustees of one of the local churches approached me to do work. I decided to offer the church and all of its members 20% off my hourly rate. They continue to be a great source of business.

Many times I'll have friends approach me to do work for them. Because they are friends I feel guilty about charging them for my work. But realistically, I can't work all day for nothing...I have bills to pay too. These same friends would have to pay someone to do the work if I didn't do it, right? The solution is to give them a great price and let them know that you are giving them a great discount.

What about weekend, holiday or overtime rates?

If you want to charge extra for weekend or holidays I suggest you charge time and a half for weekends and double time for holidays. Most customers will be comfortable with this structure since it closely matches the familiar work day environment. Will they want to pay it? Probably not, but at least they will understand the basis for the rate! Use these numbers as a starting point for negotiation.

I decided not to quote weekend or holiday rates on any printed materials or on my website. Frankly, I didn't want to advertise the fact that I might be willing to work outside of the regular Monday through Friday hours. I wanted to keep my weekends for family, rest and fun. If the customer asks, or the job demands it, I'll tell the customer that there will be a surcharge for weekends or holiday work.

I've never been successful in charging overtime rates. In every instance where I might have charged overtime I've never felt comfortable doing it. However, if I had an employee and I was paying overtime to them I would definitely pass the cost on to the customer.

Should I charge by the hour or by the job?

There is no best answer for this question. How you quote prices depends on two main factors: how confident you are about the estimate and what the customer's particular needs are.

By the job, you are taking the risk of the costs running over. In order to make this type of estimate you must be confident that you will make money at the estimated price. If the work goes smoothly you win, but if not, you will find yourself taking the loss. The more accurate you are when estimating the work to be done and the time it will take, the more money you will make. Bidding by the job has the best potential for increasing your bottom line and ironically, many customers will be more comfortable with this approach.

Bidding by the hour you'll always be safe and your compensation will exactly match the amount of time that you spend. If you're not sure how long a job will take, this is the way to protect your bottom line.

You can bid on every job that comes your way and always feel comfortable that you will be paid for the time spent. Understandably, your customers will not always be comfortable with a straight hourly estimate and will want some type of assurance that the cost will fit within their budget.

Ultimately my objective is to cover myself financially and not scare aware customers with my estimates. Sometimes I'll charge by the hour and sometimes by the job. Often I'll do both at once, charging by the hour but putting a cap on how much I think the entire job will cost. This makes the customer happy and is a safe approach for me. I will lose however, if I've set the entire job estimate too low.

To cover yourself, always add some sort of cushion to your pricing. If you think a job will take 3-4 hours to complete, quote 4-5 hours. If you think it is a $350 dollar job, quote $395 using odd pricing to your advantage.

A handyman I know quotes his rates over the telephone at $25 per hour, a low amount for our area. However, when he gets to the client's house and estimates the work to be done, he never quotes the job by the hour! He always gives them a quote for the entire job. In this way, he is never held to the low hourly rate that got him in the door. After looking over the amount of work to be done, he might quote $195 for a job he knows will only take 3-4 hours. When he finishes the work, if questioned he simply explains that he always figures in time for picking up materials, travel and clean-up.

I'm not suggesting that this is the best way to go about your business but I think it illustrates the answer to the "by the job or by the hour" question. With experience you will probably make more money quoting by the job than you will if you quote by the hour. Stand back to look at the job you are estimating and ask yourself, "How much would most people be willing to pay for this work?" If your hourly estimate will be lower than the perceived value of the work, quote it by the job at the higher price.

What if I'm not sure how long a job will take?

Experience will teach you how many hours it takes to do various jobs. In the mean time there are pricing guides available and some techniques you can use.

This book contains a guide that shows a wide range of jobs and how they were priced. You can use these for comparison purposes to price your work. If you visit my website at Handyman-Quickstart.com you'll find estimating books for sale designed for the construction industry.

Remember that estimating handyman work is not an exact science. Every task is different and every job will have unforeseen problems. Here is a technique you can use: When you're stuck, round off the job in your mind. Stop trying to figure out what the exact cost will be and start thinking in round numbers. Ask yourself if this work looks like a half day or a full day job. Will it take one day or two? This will give you a starting point for your estimate. Next, add an hour or two as a cushion.

You can also try telling your customer that you're not sure how long the work will take. Tell him that it may take as long as a full day (for example) and how much that will cost. Reassure him that you will only charge for the actual time spent. In this scenario you're working by the hour. If he insists on a firm commitment for the entire job, quote the full day rate and negotiate from there.

You're in the driver's seat. If the work is unpredictable and the client appears to be unreasonable, quote high to cover yourself. If he accepts, great! If not, move on to the next.

What if I run over? When should I charge the customer?

Be careful how and when you enter into this conversation. Your reputation is at stake.

Good communication with the homeowners throughout the course of the work will completely eliminate surprises and conflicts when you go to collect your pay. Make sure he or she understands the work being done and the challenges you are faced with.

If the over run couldn't be avoided, talk to the customer and explain what the situation was. Often, a job runs over due to unforeseen problems that crop up as you are working. If it was totally out of your control the customer should pay. If you uncover additional work to be done, show your customer as soon as possible and talk to him about the problem that faces you both. Show proof of any unexpected material costs by showing him the invoices.

If you have a good honest reason for the over run the customer will agree, or at least be willing to split the difference with you. Remember this old adage: "Volume solves all problems!" Keep your eyes on getting a referral from every customer.

Lastly, don't lose your temper! If negotiations grind to a halt and you're willing to walk away with your original estimate, just do it. Tell them that you will stand by your word. Your customer will be happy and your reputation will be intact. Ask for a referral and chalk it up to experience.

How large a deposit should I request?

There are limits on what you can request as a deposit. Check the laws in your state for the exact limits. In California, contractors are prohibited from asking for a deposit of more than 10% of the contract price or $1,000, whichever is less.

You've heard the horror stories about "tradesmen" asking for a 50% deposit and then skipping town with the money. Don't be mistaken for one of these people. If you have to request a deposit, even if you're not a contractor, follow the contractor laws for your state. Following this rule will increase your credibility and increase your chances of getting referrals.

I have chosen to never ask a customer to pay for materials in advance. I charge all of my purchases on an air miles visa card. This gives me thirty days to pay and a free round trip ticket when it comes time for a vacation. If you can, do the same.

If you don't have the available credit and the job has a large materials requirement there are solutions. Have the homeowner buy the materials so that they are on hand when you arrive. You can also go to the store together and let the homeowner choose and purchase the materials. Handled this way, the homeowner will know that they are paying nothing but cost for the materials and you will have stayed within the law. Don't ask for a large deposit.

How much should I mark up the materials that I sell?

I've always based this decision on whether or not I was being paid to pick up the materials. If I'm on the clock when I'm doing the shopping, I will not mark up the materials but will simply show them the receipt for reimbursement. Otherwise, I will mark up the materials from 10-25% over my cost. Some of the lower priced items can be marked up even further.

Can I get a contractors discount when buying materials?

Any discounts you receive have the potential of being either extra profit for you or additional savings for your customer. It's a winning situation either way so don't hesitate to ask for a discount.

I have found that the major chains have differing policies. One chain flat out said no, that they do not offer contractor discounts while another said they would sometimes discount very large purchases. That let me out on both counts!

The smaller chains and small independent hardware stores will be more willing to talk since these stores have local ownership and more flexibility due to their higher margins. They will probably be willing to give you at least 10% off. I suggest you approach them when you've got a large purchase on your cart.

Some suppliers will allow you to make purchases on account. This can be helpful for a couple of different reasons. First, this will give you 30 days to pay and maybe even a contractor's discount. But also, this account will establish a history of purchases. This history may serve as proof of experience if you choose to pursue your contractors license. Check in with a local contractors licensing school to see what steps you can take to satisfy the experience requirements.

Should I charge for mileage or travel time?

I don't charge for travel time or mileage within my normal area but many contractors do. The plumbers and electricians are particularly known for this. Check to see what other handymen in your area are doing.

When traveling outside of my normal work area I always charge for mileage and/or travel time.

If you charge for mileage, use the federal mileage rate (2008 business rate is 50.5 cents per mile). This rate was set with the intention of covering all of your vehicle expenses including gas, maintenance, insurance and depreciation.

When negotiating travel time you should use your regular hourly rate. If your customer balks at paying for the entire round trip, offer to share the burden by splitting the time.

Should I hire handyman helpers?

The hiring of employees can be a great way to increase your income as a handyman. In my area, handyman helpers would earn from $15 to $25 per hour. After figuring in payroll taxes and workman's compensation insurance the cost per hour would be closer to $25 to $35 per hour. Marking up the employee cost to $40 to $50 per hour to the client would net a profit. Multiply this number by several workers at multiple locations and it starts adding up to some real money.

Besides hiring helpers to do some of the grunt work, workers can add flexibility to your scheduling. They will enable you to overlap jobs. This is particularly helpful when jobs take longer than expected or run into additional problems. Tuesday's work can start on schedule while your worker picks up the loose ends of Monday's job. Several jobs can be started at the same time and you can leave a job site to estimate new work or to pick up additional supplies. The pool of jobs that you can take on will be bigger because you can accept more labor intensive jobs that you wouldn't normally do.

Employees create many challenges. Can you find any that are qualified? Will they be honest and dependable? Will the quality of their work be up to your standards? Will there be enough of the right type of jobs to keep them working? With the slim markups that you'll be making on employee labor hours you can't afford to have them sitting idle. Your job turns into a supervisory and a marketing position where you'll be applying your skills to meeting with new clients, estimating work, marketing your business and managing employees.

When you get to the point where you are turning away work because your schedule is full, it's time to hire some helpers and build your empire!

5 - Marketing Your Business to Earn Top Dollar for Your Services

The handyman industry needs professionals with good customer service skills. Talk to your friends and neighbors...what experiences have they had dealing with a handyman? Almost without exception you will get the same answers. "They never called back...he didn't show up. I wasted a whole day waiting for him...all I got was an answering machine, I left a message three times...the job was never finished." Unfortunately the list goes on and on.

How can I set myself apart from my competition?

It is very easy in this business to put yourself ahead of the other handymen in your area:

✓ Answer your cell phone when it rings unless you're in the middle of a conversation with a customer. Return messages the same day (or night).

- ✓ Use a hands free device. If your work is interrupted by a call, you can keep working while you talk.

- ✓ Show up on time.

- ✓ If you are running late, call the customer at or before your scheduled arrival time.

- ✓ Finish the job. Keep this as a very high priority.

- ✓ Smile and say 'Good Morning' and 'Thank-you!'

> *"If you're running late, call the customer at or before your scheduled arrival time."*

- ✓ Ask them if they are happy with your work. Use the Customer Feedback card included with your book purchase at Handyman-Quickstart.com

- ✓ Ask if they would like any other work done. Be helpful. Leave some space in your calendar for the unexpected task.

- ✓ Clearly quote the cost of a job. Avoid making vague estimates.

- ✓ Don't try to get work by being the cheapest handyman on the block. Be the best and demand to be paid as a professional.

✓ Don't ask for cash as payment or offer discounts for cash payments. Let the customer decide what form of payment to use.

✓ Be conscientious and reliable.

✓ Don't get into lengthy conversations when you're being paid to work. Keep moving and demonstrate that the time clock is important to you.

✓ Don't complain about the state of your world to a customer. Brighten their day, don't darken it.

✓ Don't talk about politics or religion.

✓ Don't make promises you can't keep.

✓ Build a network of professionals in related fields like plumbers, electricians, general contractors, roofers, carpet cleaners and painters. Refer out jobs that you can't handle or are above your legal limit.

✓ Thank people who give you referrals. Thank them again. Thank them in writing! Give them a token gift. (Flash light? Fire extinguisher?)

✓ Prepare an invoice for every job. Use the Handyman Invoice included with the purchase of this book at Handyman-Quickstart.com. Invoices are an inexpensive way to upgrade your image and set yourself apart from the competition.

✓ Keep your truck clean and organized. You'll work more efficiently and your customer will notice.

✓ Be honest. Earn their trust and ask for their referrals.

What type of customer will pay the highest rate for my services?

Millions of homeowners will agree that a good handyman is hard to find. They are afraid of calling someone they don't know from the yellow pages or classified ads. They don't want to be over charged and treated rudely only to end up with shoddy workmanship and an unfinished job. The handyman industry's negative reputation has been built by people who charge too little for their work, get overwhelmed by the workload and have no time for good customer service. Don't underestimate the opportunity that exists for a professional handyman with integrity.

> *"You can charge more than your competition if you build your business based on referrals...."*

You can charge more than your competition if you build your business based on referrals from satisfied customers. A prospective customer calling you out of the blue will usually ask first about your rates. You'll need to do a lot of sales work to build your value in their eyes before moving on to discussing rates. If you don't, you'll simply be in a bidding war with the other handymen listed in the phone book.

So which customer will pay you the highest rate? Ironically it is the customer who was referred to you. Your value went up the minute they received your business card from a friend. They will pay your rate, even if it is higher than the competition because they are confident that they are hiring a proven handyman. Now it is your job to earn the money! Building your referral network is the final key to earning top dollar for your services.

Should I advertise in the newspaper and the yellow pages?

I don't think so. Though these ads will bring you business, it is not always the type of business that you want. As I've said before, by putting your name in with all of the other handymen in your area you are entering a bidding war for work. There are better alternatives for your advertising dollar.

How can I save on newspaper advertising?

If you insist on running print ads, always test the waters with the least expensive ad you can run. Order the minimum ad run and only commit to a longer run or a larger ad after the first one has proven to be successful. Follow this advice and you will easily save the money you invested in this book many times over!

Don't forget to look online for free sources of advertising. Craigslist.com will run services ads for no charge.

Should I join a professional referral organization?

Yes. To get started in this profession you need a lot of people to know that you are a handyman. You need them to be confident that you do good work and that you are reliable and reasonably priced. You need these people to refer you to their friends and for their friends to refer you to more friends. So how do you find them without spending lots of money on advertising?

Join a referral group! I joined BNI (Business Network International) and built my entire business. You'll find other referral groups out there that operate on the same principle as BNI. LeTip International, Inc. is another popular one. There will be at least one of these referral groups in your area. To help you find them I've provided links to their home pages in the Resources and Helpful Links section at Handyman-Quickstart.com.

These groups are not free but they are worth it. BNI and LeTip are networking groups of professionals, limited to one person from each profession. They get together regularly to support each other and to trade business referrals. A networking group is exactly what you need, and may be all that you need in the way of marketing. With a good referral network you are on the road to success as a handyman.

Because they have the one person per profession rule, you will not be competing with other members of the group for business. Try to join a group that has the most power partners for your profession. Your power partners would be painters, electricians, general contractors, carpet cleaners, and other professions that offer home services and repairs or deal with seniors.

When I joined, 35 people instantly knew what I did and started to get to know me as a person. This was the start my business needed. I did work the very first week for members in the group and they gave testimonials at the next meeting praising my work.

Others members hired me and they referred me to their friends.

Success! The formula became obvious. Show up consistently at the meeting, be an active member of the group by finding as many referrals as possible for other group members, follow up on the referrals that you receive, and do a great job as a handyman.

In addition to the large number of people that quickly know who you are, there is an element from the networking group that is indispensable...people will know and trust you. You can spend money on newspaper or yellow pages ads and will probably get some calls, but people who call from these ads will not know you from Adam. They will want to know who you are, who you have done work for, if your work is any good, and if you are fairly priced. They'll ask these excellent questions because they are afraid to open up their homes to someone they don't know.

People who respond to your ad might call three other handymen and compare the services and prices of each. "Do you give free price quotes?" is a typical question. I would answer yes, of course, but I'm not anxious to get into a price war with other handymen or to waste my valuable time running around town.

People would rather deal with a handyman who has been referred to them and has proven to be trustworthy. This is where BNI and LeTip come in. The minute you were referred to this potential customer the balance tilted in your favor. You are already a trusted handyman who came highly recommended. What more could you ask for? You're two steps up the ladder of trust and you haven't even talked to them on the phone yet! When you do, you can quickly get down to the business of evaluating the job. You'll find that you are negotiating the price from a much stronger position.

The more referrals you give to members in your group, the more you will receive. "Givers Gain" is the BNI philosophy. I've referred many remodel jobs to our group's general contractor and carpet cleaning jobs to our carpet cleaner. To my customers I have become a "go to" guy for all kinds of tasks because of all the business associates in my group. In return these associates are always looking out for referrals for me.

Locally, I find that less than half of the groups have a handyman in their ranks. This means that there is a pent up demand for handyman services. Of course these groups aren't free but, when you consider that you get great referrals instead of phone calls from strangers, the dues have proven to be a genuine bargain.

What other sources of business are there?

Real estate agents are a great source of business for a handyman. The referrals that I get from them tend to be either pest repairs to complete the sale of a home, spruce up work to make a home more presentable for sale, or maintenance work on rental homes under their management. These jobs tend to have a tight time line so your prompt response will earn you their loyalty and many referrals. Real estate agents know lots of other agents and are glad to pass on your card.

The elderly are always in need of handyman work and will gladly let their friends know that they have found a good handyman. In order to effectively reach the elderly, you must get to know them. If you are active in a church let the senior ministry leader know that you are interested in offering your services to the elderly. Sponsor the church newsletter and be active in the church community.

Get to know the in-home care managers and senior care advisors in your area. They frequently need help with the installation of grab bars, wheel chair ramps and other modifications to make a home more accessible and safe for their clients.

Doing community service, being active in the PTA, coaching soccer, baseball or any activity where you are involved with groups of people will prove to be a source of referrals. Simply carry your cards with you and let people know what you do.

Should I get handyman signs for my truck?

Yes. Get magnetic signs for your truck but be careful how you advertise your business.

In California it is illegal to advertise yourself as being capable of doing a contractors work if you are not licensed. This means that you can't advertise yourself as "Joe's Painting" or "Betsy's Electric" if you're not a licensed painting or electrical contractor.

Handyman is not a licensed profession in California so I advertise myself as a Handyman, period. I have three magnetic signs on my truck. One for each door and one for the tailgate and I have gotten a lot of business from them. When I'm parked at a jobsite people will often stop to ask me what type of jobs I do and to ask for a business card.

The signs also help to identify me to my new customers when I arrive. This is another way that I set myself apart from the competition. Have you ever noticed how many workers don't have signs on their trucks? Be different but stay within the law.

Will a web page bring me more business?

I get very little handyman work from my webpage. The work that I have received came from a national commercial property management company that was looking for a local, insured handyman. Truthfully though, I don't expect my webpage to be a big source of referrals. I simply want it to confirm my credibility and show off my work.

Most of the visitors to my site have already heard about me and were given my card (which is where they found my web address). When they visit the site they will see examples of my work before they call. I don't list prices, instead I focus on the jobs that I have done and am available to do.

Handyman Pricing Guide

How Much Should I Charge For...?

Creating an estimating guide for a handyman is a real challenge! No two handyman jobs are identical and most jobs have hidden problems that add to the cost. To further confuse the process is that local pricing for labor and materials vary as do building code requirements.

This pricing guide quotes jobs based on July 2008 prices. Because inflation is consistently pushing prices upward, you may be able to charge more than the guide will suggest. This is particularly true if skilled labor is hard to find in your area.

Pricing handyman work is a lot different than pricing an auto repair. In the automobile industry they use a book to set labor rates. That book is relying on the fact that every Chevy Malibu that needs repair should require the same amount of labor to change out the alternator. If variations arise from modifications to the car, the mechanic will charge for the extra time at the shop's going rate.

So how do I create a meaningful pricing guide? I've decided to base the information on actual jobs that I have done with the price that I would charge if I were doing the job today. With photos of the jobs being discussed, this is the closest thing to coming to the job site with me and talking about the work first hand.

Several assumptions apply:

- The labor hours given for a particular job are based on the job going smoothly with few if any unexpected difficulties.

- The worker is of average ability, is reasonably experienced in the job at hand and is motivated to complete the work in a reasonable amount of time.

- In virtually all cases you will have to make some modifications to the labor estimate to fit your particular skills and the specifics of the job.

- The "Total Invoice Amounts" quoted are for the jobs pictured including labor at an average rate of $50 per hour.

Consider these estimates to be a suggestion only. They are presented in the hope that they will serve as a starting point to determining your own pricing.

Indoor Maintenance, Repairs And Installations:

Air Conditioner: Window Installation

The home has a thick layer of stucco siding. A little extra time was spent in fashioning a custom support bracket to replace the manufacturer's flimsy bracket.

Items to consider: Is there a sufficient electrical source nearby? What is the condition of the window sill?

Labor: 3 hours

Total invoice including materials: $185

Baseboard Installation: Bathroom

This bathroom had been recently painted and the homeowner wanted new base board installed. The bathroom is approximately 7 by 12 feet and has slightly rounded corners. A final coat of paint was applied to the baseboard.

Items to consider: Will you be painting the baseboard? Are the corners rounded?

Labor: 3 hours

Total invoice including materials: $205

Closet Shelving System Design and Installation

This hall closet needed some shelving to make the space more efficient. The original shelf was left in place and used to help secure the new shelving. After installing the shelves, the clothes rod was cut down to fit the new width.

Items to consider: How much tear out needs to be done to clear the closet? Who will do the painting in the closet where old supports or shelves have been removed? Do you want the shelves to be adjustable?

Labor: 2 - 3 hours

Total invoice including materials: $175

Door Pull Installation

Looks like a small job but upon closer consideration you realize how much goes into installing door pulls.

You can't do this work on a door in place because the router creates too much dust. Do the work in a garage or outdoors.

These doors were 8 feet tall and custom built. Being very expensive, there was no room for error. Having the correct bit and setting up the router jig was the most important step. Because there were 14 doors to be done the time spent in creating the jig was recouped and the work became more efficient as the job neared completion.

Items to consider: Include time to create a jig for the router, the cost of the router bid and time to remove and reinstall doors.

Labor: 1 hour for a single door

Total invoice including materials: $500 for 14 doors

Dry Rot: Bathroom Repairs

Are the floor joists also damaged? This job did not include the cost of new floor coverings.

Because of leaky toilet seals, pest inspectors often find dry rot in the sub-flooring beneath the toilet area. The

cost to repair this type of damage will vary greatly depending on the extent of the damage and the type of flooring. In this case, the damage was limited to the corner of the floor between the toilet and the tub. The picture shows the work with new sub-flooring in place. Once the floor joists were inspected and found to be in sound condition new sub-flooring was installed and caulked. The original vinyl flooring was then glued back down and the toilet re-installed with new wax ring.

Items to consider: Will new flooring be installed or the will the old floor covering be preserved? What condition are the floor joists in? Are the joists supporting the waste collar in solid condition?

Labor: 4 – 5 hours

Total invoice including materials: $325

Drywall Repairs: Patching Holes

In the center of this picture there was a 5" circular hole in the sheetrock made by the homeowner's head when he took a fall. Ouch.

Texture from a spray can was used along with fast drying joint compound and a hair dryer to speed surface drying.

Items to consider: How many trips will have to be made? Will you be doing the final painting?

Labor: 1 ½ hours

Total invoice including materials: $100

Electrical: Attic Ventilator Replacement

This particular job was for the replacement of a gable end attic ventilation fan that had worn out bearings.

With easy attic access and the electrical supply already in place this installation went smoothly.

Items to consider: If this is a new installation, is electricity available? What is the size of the gable end vent?

Labor: 1 - 2 hours

Total invoice including materials: $175

Electrical: Bathroom Exhaust Fan Installation

This was a new installation. Electricity was available from the nearby GFCI protected circuit. A switch box was added and the wiring dropped through the wall. After the wiring was completed the installation of the fan itself was relatively easy. The exhaust tubing was routed through the nearby gable end of the house.

Items to consider: Will the exhaust tubing be routed through the roof or through a gable end? Is the circuit protected by a GFCI and installed up to code requirements?

Labor: 5 hours

Total invoice including materials: $350

Electrical: Ceiling Fan Installation

No additional wiring was needed and the electrical box was rated for a ceiling fan.

Items to consider: What is the condition of the existing electrical box? How complex is the fan assembly and does the fan have a light? If you will be upgrading to a ceiling fan rated electrical box, add at least 1 hour.

Labor: 1 to 1 ½ hours

Total invoice including materials: $85

Electrical: Receptacle Replacement

The particular job I'm quoting here involved the replacement of all 22 duplex receptacles throughout the house.

Items to consider: What is the condition of the existing wiring? Is there a grounding wire present or is the metallic box grounded? To avoid giving the impression that a ground is present, never install a conventional three-wire grounding receptacle on a circuit that does not provide an equipment ground. Check building codes in your area.

Labor: 15 minutes per outlet

Total invoice including materials: $350

Electrical: Light Fixture Replacement

Replaced an old fashioned external fixture with this contemporary fixture.

Items to consider: Is the existing box grounded and able to receive the new fixture? Will any unpainted areas be left exposed after the installation of the new fixture?

Labor: 30 minutes per fixture

Total invoice not including light fixture: $50

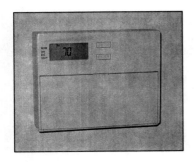

Electrical: Thermostat (Room) Replacement

Replaced an old circular mercury thermostat with a new electronic thermostat with timer.

Items to consider: Compatibility with existing furnace and/or air conditioner. Disposal of the old thermostat should be done in conformance with local laws. Most early thermostats contain Mercury, a hazardous substance.

Labor: 20 minutes

Total invoice including thermostat: $75

Electrical: Track Lighting Installation

This installation replaced an existing ceiling light. The existing electrical box was covered and wiring was run from that box to the new location for the track light. No additional switches were needed.

Items to consider: Is there an existing fixture that is being replaced? If not, is there electricity available nearby? Is a permit needed for the wiring?

Labor: 1 – 2 hours

Total invoice including track light: $145

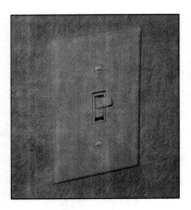

Electrical: Wall Switch Replacement

This was part of a larger job. The amount of time required to replace a light switch is usually minimal, averaging any where from 5 to 15 minutes per switch.

Items to consider: Local building codes. Purchase the best quality switch available.

Labor: 5 - 15 minutes per switch

Grab Bar Installation

Grab bars are often installed at entry ways, near steps, in bathrooms and in shower/bath enclosures. This client wanted two bars on the front porch.

Items to consider: Grab bars need to be attached to framing members for stability. In showers and bath enclosures they are often installed at a 45 degree angle for safety and to make them more useful when rising on reclining. Keep plenty of fastening hardware available: everything from stainless steel screws to molly bolts.

Labor: 30 minutes per grab bar

Total invoice including materials: $125

Hanging Mirrors and Shelves

This type of job is usually done as a part of a larger job. Though simple to accomplish the majority of your time is spent measuring, leveling and working with the homeowner on location.

Items to consider: What other jobs does the homeowner need done? You'll do a lot of this type work. Carry with you every type of wall fastener and picture hanger available.

Labor: ½ - 1 hour

Total invoice: $65

Lockers: Design and Build

The homeowner wanted 4 lockers built. The lower  storage area is for shoes and various sport items. The shelf is placed using a dado joint and strengthened with "L" brackets to allow it to be used as a seat. Hooks are included above for hanging jackets, back packs and sport uniforms.

Design time, shopping time, laying out the work, routing the dado joints, installing adjustable feet, priming, painting and delivery all added up to about 12 hours labor to build 4 lockers.

Items to consider: This is the type of job that can be done at your shop then transported to the site. Whose design will it be? What grade of materials will you use?

Labor: 4 hours for one

Total invoice including materials: $850 for 4

Lockset Replacement

Out with the old and in with the new. This lockset required that an additional hole be drilled at the bottom of the handle.

Items to consider: Condition of the door and the jamb. When installing lock sets all of the new hardware should be installed, including the jamb hardware. Will any chiseling need to be done to fit the hardware into the door? Purchasing better quality hardware will save on installation time.

Labor: 15 minutes per lockset

Total invoice including materials: $125

Office Furniture Assembly

This was a four piece set. The desk was sectional with a book case, filing cabinet and printer stand.

Items to consider: The first piece of furniture takes longer than the rest because it takes time to figure out the manufacturer's scheme. Who will dispose of the substantial amount of packaging materials?

Labor: 1 – 2 hours per piece

Total invoice: $200 for 4 pieces

Painting: Room

This was a two tone paint job plus the ceiling in a 12' x 15' room. Pictures were hung and furniture replaced after the paint had dried. Extra cutting was required because 3 different colors were used. This job was painted with roller and brush.

Items to consider: Half to two thirds of your time will be spent moving furniture, filling holes in the wall, taping corners and trim, removing or taping fixtures and laying drop cloths. Purchase the best quality paint available for more efficient coverage. Consider using a tinted primer for the initial coat.

Labor: 3 hours per 100 square feet of wall space

Total invoice including materials: $450

Painting: Refinish Furniture

Sanding, varnishing and installing new hardware. The basic finish was in good condition. It had some very

ugly colonial style handles that had been installed upside down. They were removed and the drill holes filled.

Items to consider: This could be a 1 hour cleanup job or a multi-hour restoration. For a small cabinet in need of TLC, I charge by the hour. For heavier refinishing, clients will expect to pay by the job.

Labor: 1 to 4 hours per piece

Total invoice including materials: $130

Plumbing: Faucet Replacement

This was an installation of a new faucet into a new granite counter.

Items to consider: Is there adequate space under the sink for the nuts that secure the faucet in place? How is the access? Best practice is to replace the water supply lines at the same time as the faucet.

Labor: 45 minutes

Total invoice excluding materials: $50

Plumbing: Garbage Disposer Replacement

Replacing a garbage disposal has its challenges. Removing the old hardware and cleaning up the bottom of the sink, sealing the new disposer in place and replacing all hoses pretty much sums it up.

Items to consider: Is the outlet that the disposer plugs into protected by a GFCI? How is the rest of the drain assembly?

Labor: 1 hour

Total invoice excluding materials: $50

Plumbing: Refrigerator Ice Maker Hookup

This customer's old refrigerator had no ice maker. When the new refrigerator was purchased a water line needed to be run. Accessing cold water under the sink, the copper line was run down through the cabinet, under the floor (approximately 12') and up through the floor behind the refrigerator.

Items to consider: Figure in extra tubing above the floor to allow the refrigerator to be pulled out for access.

Labor: 2 hours

Total invoice including materials: $175

Smoke Detector Installation

This is an A/C powered smoke/carbon monoxide alarm combination model. The A/C wiring was already in place. This home has its original 35 year old forced air furnace. Because of the age of the furnace the client was concerned about the increasing possibility of a furnace failure causing a carbon monoxide hazard.

Items to consider: If you are replacing an existing smoke alarm, be sure to locate the new alarm in the same location as the original. If no alarms are present in the house check local codes for location requirements. Plan for the time spent laying out the locations of the alarms.

Labor: 15 minutes each

Total invoice including materials: $75

Water Heater Strapping Installation

Water heater strapping for earthquake safety is a code requirement in California. Always choose the best  grade strapping available. The water heater pictured was installed right up against the corner. No extra blocking was required to secure it.

Items to consider: Are studs available and within reach to secure strapping? Many water heaters are in tiny closets with limited access to the back wall studs. Keep at it, I haven't found a water heater yet that couldn't be secured.

Labor: 1 hour

Total invoice including materials: $80

Outdoor Maintenance, Repairs And Installations:

Caulk Exterior of Home

Caulking the exterior of a home can be very time consuming. Typically all joints where dissimilar materials come together including all locations where window or door-trim meet siding are caulked.

Items to consider: Check the roof top for penetrations that may be ready for fresh caulk. Will any old caulk need to be removed? What type of caulk will be used? What color will the caulk be?

Labor: 3 hours per 1,500 Sq. Ft.

Total invoice including caulk for 2,200 Sq. Ft: $275

Chicken Coop

Will the variety never end? Let's hope not, this was simply a fun project. My client wanted a chicken coop to keep his 4 hens safe and contained. Final dimensions were approximately 4' x 3' x 4' tall. Constructed mostly out of scrap lumber, costs were kept to a minimum with only the 1" chicken wire, the hardware and the corrugated roofing sheet being purchased new.

Items to consider: Whose design will it be? Design considerations: A roost, a box for nesting, a entry door for the birds at ground level, hinges for the roof for easy access and an earthen floor to manage the accumulation of straw and droppings.

Labor: 4 hours

Total invoice including materials: $300

Dry Rot: Doorsill Repairs

These are before and after pictures. We opted to repair the door jamb where dry rot was present and install a new doorsill. The new doorsill was installed first. Next, using fast hardening epoxy wood filler, the gaping hole in the jamb was repaired and sanded to blend.

Items to consider: Repair vs. replacement of the trim. How easily is the old sill removed? Who will do the painting?

Labor: 3 hours

Total invoice including materials: $195

Dry Rot: Exterior Trim Repairs

The pest inspector found dry rot on this trim board. Should the entire trim board be replaced or should the repair be made with wood filler? I filled it with epoxy wood filler which dries hard in 20 minutes.

Items to consider: In this case it was easier to fill the repair then to replace the trim board. In addition to the time needed to find matching trim it would have also required more priming and painting than simply repairing the existing trim.

Labor: 1 hour

Total invoice including wood filler: $85

Dry Rot: Siding Replacement

The siding under this window was damaged by dry rot. The siding was replaced, caulked and primed ready for paint. The air conditioner support needed to be removed and reinstalled. The entire window trim was re-caulked to prevent further damage.

Items to consider: Is matching siding available? Can the cause of the damage be determined and corrected? Who will do the painting? This house was about to be painted so only a primer coat was needed.

Labor: 2 – 3 hours

Total invoice including materials: $145

Dry Rot: Under Sink Repairs

The plumbing had been leaking and the wood was badly damaged. After clearing out the old wood, a structure is added to support the cabinet bottom. Exterior/wet grade plywood followed by primer and paint created a lasting surface.

Items to consider: How much damage has been done by leaking water? Is there damage to the sub-flooring under the cabinet?

Labor: 2 – 3 hours

Total invoice including materials: $175

Dry Rot: Window Trim Replacement

The pest inspector found dry rot on this window trim. The trim board at the bottom of the window was replaced, caulked and primed.

Items to consider: Is there any damage other than the trim? Can the source of the damage be located and corrected? Who will apply the final paint color?

Labor: 1 hour

Total invoice including materials: $75

Fence Repairs: Add Privacy Panels

The homeowner wanted to freshen up the look of the fence and increase the privacy that the fence provides. After checking the fence boards and posts to be sure they were secure, vertical supports were added followed by the redwood lattice.

Items to consider: What is the condition of the fence? Are there height restrictions to consider? What grade of lattice will be used?

Labor: 3 – 4 hours

Total invoice including materials: $310

Fence Repairs: Adding Sections

The fence posts were in good shape but the rest of the boards were falling apart. Many of the old boards were missing or damaged. The homeowner decided that she wanted all new boards. The old materials had to be hauled away and disposed of.

Items to consider: What is the condition of the rest of the fence? Can any of the old materials be salvaged? Often recycled wood is better quality than new and is worth saving.

Labor: 6 hours

Total invoice including materials: $500

Fence Repairs: Build and Install a Gate

Homeowner wanted a new gate for the sidewalk leading to her garden. The materials were redwood with new gate hardware.

Items to consider: What condition are the adjacent posts in? Is the walkway level? Building a strong gate that will not sag is the challenge.

Labor: 3 hours

Total invoice including materials: $220

Fence Repairs: Fence Post Replacement

The original redwood fence post was rotted away at the bottom. The challenge in replacing an existing fence post is the block of concrete that is left in the ground. Either the block needs to be removed or a new post hole dug adjacent to it. In this case, the old post was pulled out of the concrete leaving a 12" deep hole...very convenient! The new post was inserted into the old concrete and an additional 10" of concrete was added to bring the concrete up above ground level.

Items to consider: Every failed post has a reason. In this case the level of the original concrete was well below ground level allowing the base of the post to be in contact with the soil. Fencing repairs where concrete is added will always require 2 trips. One to set the concrete and the second to complete the repair after the concrete has cured.

Labor: 3 hours

Total invoice including materials: $175

Front Door Replacement

This door is old and damaged. The existing door is standard sized at 3'0" by 6'8". The homeowner will do the finish painting.

New hardware will be installed. The sill and the interior trim are in good condition.

Items to consider: Purchasing a slab door and preparing the door for hardware versus purchasing a pre-hung door and removing and replacing the door trim is the most important question. How are your skills at drilling out a slab door to accept hardware? What is the condition of the existing trim both inside and out? How much damage will be done to the trim if you remove the entire door frame to install a pre-hung door?

Labor: 3 - 4 hours

Total invoice including materials: $350

Gutter Guard Installation

This picture shows new gutter guard installed on an aluminum seamless gutter. The leaf guard used is made of aluminum and comes in 20' rolls. After cleaning leaves out of the gutters the guard is installed. In this case, the guard is pushed up under the bottom course of shingles and is then attached to the front of the gutter with sheet metal screws.

Items to consider: How much time will be spent cleaning the gutters out to prepare for the installation? What is the condition of the gutter? This is a great time to seal any leaking seams in the gutter.

Labor: 3 hours for 175' of gutter.

Total invoice including materials: $200

Mailbox Installation

The original mailbox was knocked over by a car. This mailbox installation included digging a new hole and installing the post in concrete. After installing the post  a second trip was needed to install the mailbox and paint the post.

Items to consider: When considering the cost of a job like this, removal of the old concrete can add significantly to the time required. Is there an alternative location for the mailbox? Don't forget to consult postal regulations regarding height and location of the box.

Labor: 3 hours

Total invoice including materials: $175

Painting: Front Porch and Steps

This porch and steps are made of wood and the old paint was peeling. The porch is about 4' x 6' in size. These usually require pressure washing or sanding, priming and painting.

Items to consider: This job required a lot of sanding and some wood filler. When the steps were being painted, cutting in the steps required extra time.

Labor: 3 ½ hours

Total invoice including materials: $225

Painting: Re-Stain Deck

To re-stain these decks, the biggest block of time was spent preparing for the stain. Pressure washing the decks and repairing the rotted and broken boards needed to be completed first.

Items to consider: Allow 48 hours for a wooden deck to dry after pressure washing. Will you charge a fee for the pressure washer? What types of repairs are needed before staining? Could you hire a helper to do some of the prep work?

Labor: 3 – 6 hours

Total invoice including materials and pressure washing fee: $450

Pressure Wash a Driveway

This "before" picture of a driveway shows plenty of fungus blackening the concrete surface. The driveway is 20 feet long by 20 feet wide.

Pricing for pressure washing is a function of the size of the job, what type of surface you will be cleaning and whether chemicals will be used.

Items to consider: Will you use hot or cold water? Will you be applying a detergent? Will you charge a fee for the pressure washer? I charge a $45 pressure washer fee in addition to my regular hourly rate. Chemicals are extra.

Labor: 1 hour for 20' x 20' area

Total invoice including $45 pressure washer fee: $95

Railing: Build and Install for Spa Steps

The railing on the left was built by another handyman but the clients weren't happy with it. They wanted something more attractive and more stable. Redwood was their preferred material and they wanted a grab bar added to the middle of the step. This wouldn't have been my first choice for the location of the bar but it is, or course, their decision.

Items to consider: What materials will be used? Usually the design collaboration is between the handyman and the homeowner.

Labor: 6 hours

Total invoice including materials: $485

Railing for Garage Steps

Install a simple hand rail, primed and painted.

Built out of sanded redwood, this rail is simple and functional. The vertical post is firmly mounted with galvanized brackets and concrete screws into both the concrete step and the floor. No screw heads are exposed on the top rail. The finished railing is primed and ready for paint.

Items to consider: Keeping the wiggle out of the railing without building it like Fort Knox.

Labor: 1 - 2 hours

Total invoice including materials: $165

Screen Door Installation

Installing a screen door is usually pretty straight forward. You choose the correct size for the opening and screw it in...but not always.

Items to consider: Be aware of conflicts between the knob on the screen door and the existing knob. Latch alignment can sometimes be tricky. The trim around every door seems to be different. Is the existing trim ready to receive a screen door?

Labor: 1 – 2 hours per door

Shutter Installation

The appearance of this home was upgraded by the installation of these cosmetic metal shutters. Because the home had stucco siding, it took some extra time to attach the shutters.

Items to consider: Figure some extra time to plan the location of the shutters. Should they be flush up against the window frame or adjacent to the trim? What is the siding material? Plan on weather sealing the holes where the screws penetrate the siding.

Labor: 1 ½ hours

Total invoice for labor only: $100

Stairway Replacement for a Deck

The steps in the top picture failed because the foot of the stringer was resting on bare earth. When the wood rotted away, the steps crumbled. To install these properly, concrete footings needed to be added at the bottom of the steps. The lower post for the railing was sunk into concrete to provide extra stability for the steps and railing.

This job required two trips to complete. The first trip was to remove the old steps and to prepare and pour the concrete for the railing post. The second trip was to build the steps. The railing and the step surface materials were built using recycled redwood.

Items to consider: How many steps are there? Is there any concrete work to be done? Can you use pre-cut stringers or will you lay-out and cut your own?

Labor: 7 hours

Total invoice including materials: $475

Threshold Installation

This new home did not have its thresholds installed. An aluminum model was installed on the concrete floor. Caulk was added under the threshold and at both ends.

Items to consider: How easily will the original threshold be removed? What type of threshold is needed? Don't forget to check the weather stripping around the door.

Labor: 1 hour

Total invoice including materials: $90

Trailer Bed Replacement

This small trailer was worth repairing. It is approximately 6' wide by 7' long and is capable of carrying small farm equipment. Using pressure treated 2x6 Fir and securing the planks with round headed carriage bolts, this trailer is ready to go. To complicate the installation the planks slid under both the front and rear supports before securing.

Items to consider: Removal of the old bed took longer than planned because there were plenty of rusted bolts to be cut off.

Labor: 4 hours

Total invoice including materials: $285

Tubular Skylight Installation

This could be the perfect retrofit to brighten up dark areas of a home. We are often asked to install tubular skylights.

Items to consider: Be sure your liability insurance covers roofing installations and repairs. For multiple installations, $125 - $175 labor per skylight is common. If working on a tile roof, you can usually charge an additional $175.

Labor: 2 ½ hours for two skylights

Total invoice including the skylights: $500

Wheelchair Ramps: Build and Install

This front walk had two 6 inch steps that needed wheelchair ramps. This job was trickier then it first appeared. To make a smooth ramp and avoid tripping points the measurements were  precise and the ramp's leading plywood edges were tapered.

Using exterior grade plywood and 2″ x 6″ support joists these ramps were secured to the walkway with concrete screws. They were then primed and painted. The weather was hot and dry so the entire job was completed in a single trip.

Items to consider: Allow extra time for designing the ramp, securing it in place, priming, painting and applying a non-skid surface.

Labor: 3 – 4 hours

Total invoice including materials: $280

"An investment
in knowledge
always pays the
best interest."

Ben Franklin

Made in the USA